English Smart 2

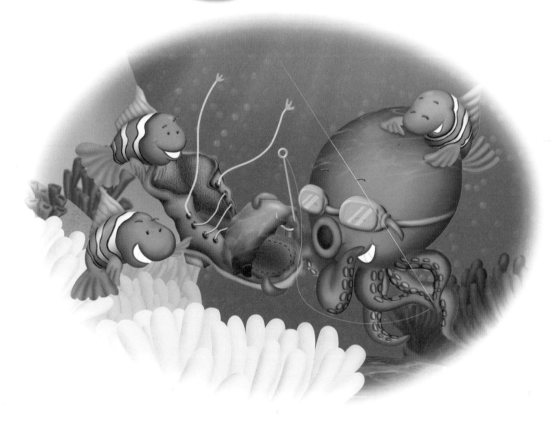

Marilyn Kennedy

ISBN : 1-894810-88-0

Printed in China

Contents

Grade 2

The Bumblebee

The bumblebee is an insect. It is yellow and black and has six legs. Most bumblebees live in a group in a nest. Each group or colony has a queen, worker bees, and drones. The queen is the leader.

The queen bee lays 4 to 8 eggs in the nest after a winter in hibernation. These eggs hatch to become worker bees and drones. The colony grows until it has 50 to 600 bees. The worker bees help make new plants grow and they make honey from the nectar in flowering plants.

A. Read the story and answer the questions.

1. What kind of animal is a bumblebee?

    _____

2. What colour is a bumblebee?

    _____

3. Who is the leader of the bumblebee colony?

    _____

4. When does the queen bee lay her eggs?

    _____

Phonics: Beginning Consonants

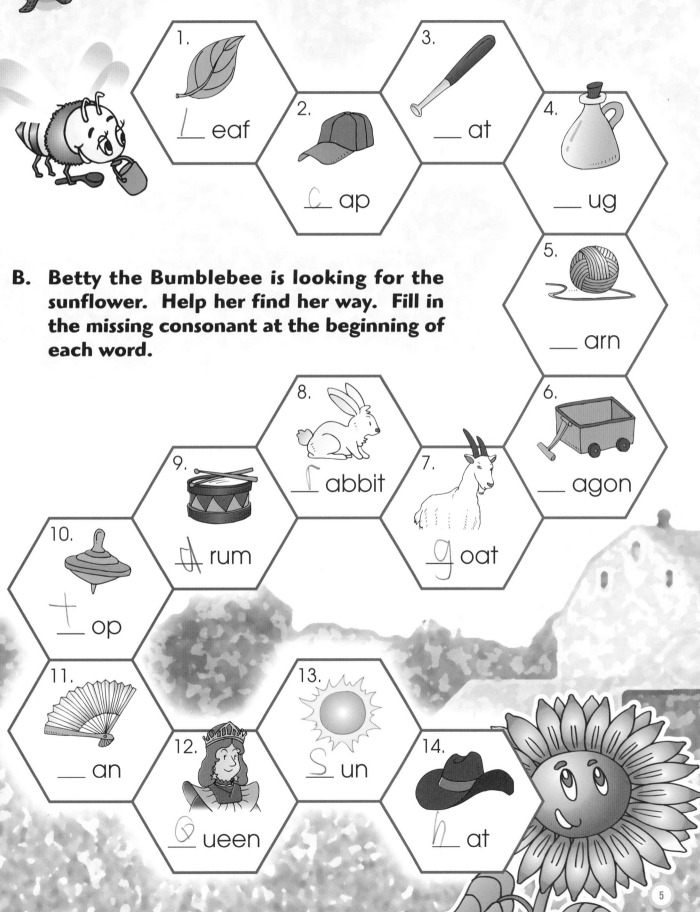

1. <u>L</u> eaf

2. <u>C</u> ap

3. ___ at

4. ___ ug

5. ___ arn

B. Betty the Bumblebee is looking for the sunflower. Help her find her way. Fill in the missing consonant at the beginning of each word.

6. ___ agon

7. <u>g</u> oat

8. <u>r</u> abbit

9. <u>d</u> rum

10. <u>t</u> op

11. ___ an

12. <u>Q</u> ueen

13. <u>S</u> un

14. <u>h</u> at

Sentence Recognition

- A **Sentence** is a group of words that tells a complete thought about someone or something.

C. Underline the groups of words that are not complete sentences.

1. Polar bears live in the Arctic. They are big and white. Big paws. They have small eyes and ears. Jump from ice floe to ice floe.

2. Polar bears have other names. Sometimes called white bears, sea bears, or ice bears. Swim very well.

3. Polar bears move fast and travel far. Eat seals and fish. The male is usually larger than the female. Hairy feet.

4. Baby bears or cubs are born in winter. Weigh 2 pounds when born. Remain with mothers from 10 months to 2 years.

Code Word Game

D.   Help Tim use the code below to read the sentences.

A	B	C	D	E	F	G	H	I	J	K	L	M	N	O
1	2	3	4	5	6	7	8	9	10	11	12	13	14	15

P	Q	R	S	T	U	V	W	X	Y	Z
16	17	18	19	20	21	22	23	24	25	26

1.   A   S Q U A R E
     1   19 17 21 1' 18 5

     I S   A   S H A P E
     9 19 1   19 8 1 16 5

     W S T H   F O U R
     23 9 20 8 6 15 21 18

     E Q U A L
     5 17 21 1 12

     S I D E S .
     19 9 4 5 19

2.   A   T R I A N G L E
     1   20 18 9 1 14 7 12 5

     I S   A   S H A P E
     9 19 1   19 8 1 16 5

     _ I T _   T _ R _ _
     23 9 20 8 20 8 18 5 5

     S I D E S .
     19 9 4 5 19

3.

     _ _ _ _ _ _ _
     1   3 9 18 3 12 5

     _ _ _   _ _ _ _ _ _
     9 19 1   19 9 14 7 12 5

     _ _ _ _ .
     12 9 14 5

4.   _ _ _ _ _ _ _ _ _ _
     1   18 5 3 20 1 14 7 12 5

     _ _ _   _ _ _ _ _
     9 19 1   19 8 1 16 5

     _ _ _ _
     23 9 20 8

     _ _ _ _ _ _ _ _
     15 16 16 15 19 9 20 5

     _ _ _ _ _   _ _ _ _ _
     19 9 4 5 19   20 8 1 20

     _ _ _   _ _ _ _ _ _ .
     1 18 5   5 17 21 1 12

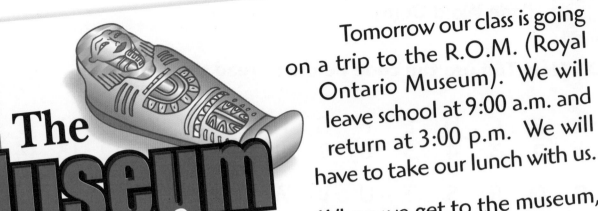

The Museum Trip

Tomorrow our class is going on a trip to the R.O.M. (Royal Ontario Museum). We will leave school at 9:00 a.m. and return at 3:00 p.m. We will have to take our lunch with us.

When we get to the museum, we will visit the Bat Cave, the dinosaurs, and the Egyptian mummies.

The day after our trip, when we get back to school, we will draw pictures and write about what we saw there.

ROM
Royal Ontario Museum

A. Circle the correct answers.

1. What is the story about?

   A. visiting the school   B. a trip to the museum
   C. looking at dinosaurs

2. What will the children take with them?

   A. snacks   B. lunch   C. a school bag

3. Which of these will they see?

   A. paintings   B. mummies   C. toys

4. What will they do after the trip?

   A. play a game   B. watch a movie   C. draw pictures

Phonics: Middle and Ending Consonants

B. Look at the pictures. Fill in the missing consonants.

1 bu __s__

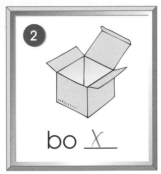

2 bo __x__

3 nes __t__

4 di __ __ e

5 tuli __

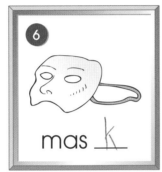

6 mas __k__

7 ba __

8 po __t__

9 pe __

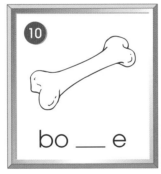

10 bo __ e

11 ca __

12 bal __

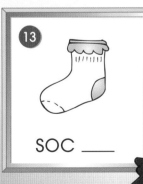

13 soc __

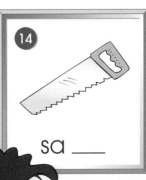

14 sa __

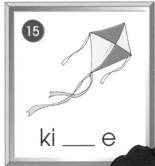

15 ki __ e

16 ra __ e

 Subject of a Sentence

- The **Subject** part of a sentence tells whom or what the sentence is about.

C. Look at the pictures. Write a subject for each sentence.

1. _____ are my favourite fruit.

2. _____ is the tallest self-supporting tower in the world.

3. _____ rotates around the sun.

4. _____ has a monitor and a keyboard.

5. _____ is my favourite sport.

6. _____ is 8:15 a.m.

7. Draw and write.

_____ is what I like to do with friends.

Alike and Different

- You can compare things by looking at how they are alike and how they are different. If two things are **alike**, something about them is the same. If two things are **different**, something about them is not the same.

D. **Read the sentences. Put a check mark ✔ in the box to indicate the sport being described.**

	Hockey	Baseball
1. We play it on ice.		
2. We play it on a field.		
3. Something is hit.		
4. There are goalposts.		
5. Players run.		
6. Players wear skates.		
7. Players wear caps.		
8. Scores are kept.		

The Eurotunnel

Have you heard of the Eurotunnel? It is the longest undersea tunnel in the world. We can travel from England to France through this tunnel.

The idea of a tunnel running under the English Channel is not new. As early as 1802, a French engineer tried to convince the emperor Napolean to build one. In 1993, it was finally built.

The Eurotunnel actually consists of three tunnels: one for trains that carry people in one direction and another for trains to carry people in the opposite direction. A third service tunnel allows fresh air, repair workers, and emergency vehicles to reach the train tunnels.

A. Answer the questions.

1. Which countries are linked by the Eurotunnel?

_____

2. When was the Eurotunnel built?

_____

3. Who was the French emperor in 1802?

_____

4. Why are there three tunnels?

_____

Phonics: Short Vowels

B. **Rob is looking for the tunnel. Help him find his way. Fill in the missing vowels a, e, i, o, or u.**

14. r __ ck

13. t __ nt

12. f __ n

1. l __ mp

15. s __ x

11. l __ ps

2. w __ b

16. n __ t

10. c __ n

3. m __ p

9. n __ t

4. j __ g

5. p __ t

6. b __ g

7. d __ sk

8. b __ ll

 Predicate of a Sentence

- The **Predicate** is the part of the sentence that tells what the subject is doing.

C. Write a predicate for each sentence.

1. In spring, flowers _____ _____ .

2. In summer, we _____ _____ .

3. In fall, I _____ _____ .

4. In winter, I _____ _____ .

5. My favourite sport _____ _____ .

6. On Mother's Day, we _____ _____ .

7. In my dream, I _____ _____ .

8. My family _____ _____ .

Classification / Grouping

D. **Louise the Ladybug wants to sort some words. Write the words that belong to each group under the first word.**

> cup   blackboard   desk   swing   eraser
>
> seesaw   pear   bowl   slide   tires   horn
>
> grapes   apple   glass   key

1. cupboard

_____

_____

_____

2. school

_____

_____

_____

3. car

_____

_____

_____

4. playground

_____

_____

_____

5. fruit

_____

_____

_____

Snakes

A. Jake the Snake needs help to finish the story. Fill in the missing words for him.

Snakes are 1._____ that have 2._____ , slender bodies. They have no limbs. They are 3._____ -blooded because they have a low body temperature.

Snakes are non-mammals because they lay 4._____ , which hatch soon after they are 5._____ . They go into 6._____ , or a kind of sleep, for part of the year. Snakes shed their 7._____ several times a year. They 8._____ by slithering from one 9._____ to another.

cold   laid   long
eggs   reptiles
hibernation   move
skins   place

Phonics: Long Vowels

B. Help Jeff the Snake look for his friend. Fill in the blanks with a, i, o, or u.

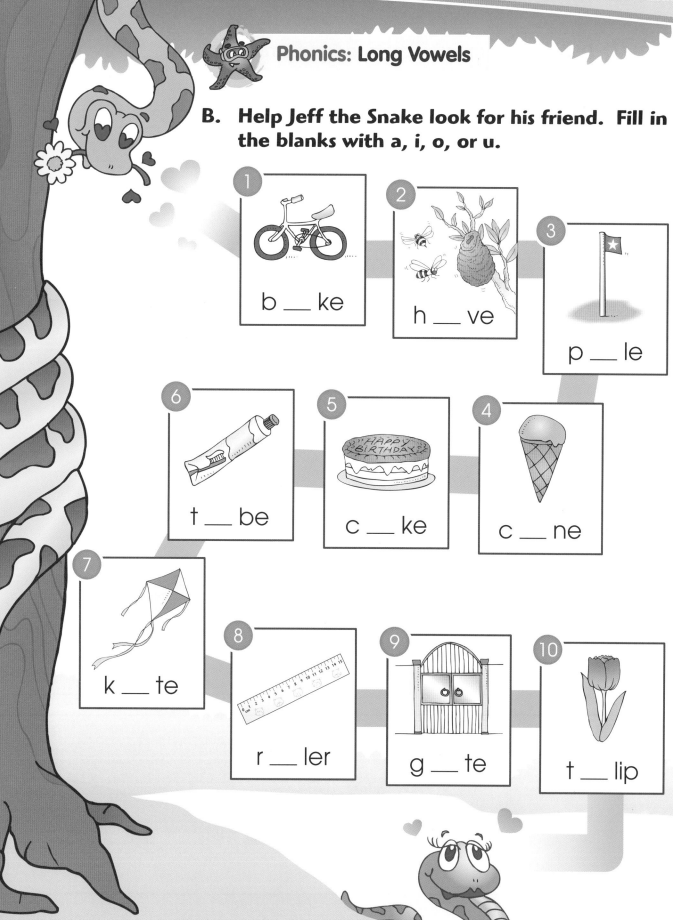

1. b __ ke

2. h __ ve

3. p __ le

4. c __ ne

5. c __ ke

6. t __ be

7. k __ te

8. r __ ler

9. g __ te

10. t __ lip

Distinguishing Subjects and Predicates

- A sentence has two main parts – a **Subject** and a **Predicate**.
- The **Subject** tells whom or what the sentence is about.
- The **Predicate** tells what is happening.

C. **Match the subjects with the predicates. Write the sentences on the lines below.**

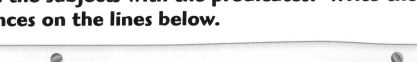

Subject	Predicate
At the zoo, we	helps clean the cages.
The monkey	has a mane on its neck.
The African elephant	is black and white.
The zebra	likes to hang by its tail.
The male lion	visit the animals.
The tiger	is orange and black.
The zookeeper	is the largest living land animal.

1. At the zoo we visit the animals.

2. The monkey likes to hang by its tail

3. The African elephant is the largest living land animal.

4. The zebra is black and white.

5. The male lion has a mane on its neck.

6. The tiger is orange and black.

7. The zookeeper helps clean the cages.

Context Clues

D. Read the story. Use the boldfaced words to fill in the blanks.

Cooking with Mom

Mom and I took out the **recipe** for Rice Krispie Cookies from the recipe **box**. The **ingredients** included rice krispies, marshmallows, and butter. We got the rice krispies and marshmallows from the **cupboard** and the butter from the **refrigerator**.

We heated the butter in a **pot** on the **stove**. When the butter was **melted**, we added the marshmallows. Then we stirred in the rice krispies. Lastly, we scooped the mixture out of the bowl and into a **square** pan.

1. A _____ gives directions for cooking.

2. My brother keeps his toys in a _____ .

3. The _____ are the things used in cooking something.

4. We often keep dry ingredients in a _____ .

5. I store butter in a _____ .

6. You can heat something in a _____ on a _____ until it is _____ .

7. Our cookie mixture went into a _____ pan.

Jane went out to play. She called on her friend, Sarah, but she wasn't at home. Then she went to Christine's house, but she wasn't at home either. Jane felt sad. There was no one to play with.

What Happens Next?

A. Write what you think will happen next. Give the story to a friend and ask him/her to write his/her ideas beside yours.

Your ideas	Your friend's ideas

Phonics: **Vowel Digraphs - ai and ay**

B. Find the words with "ai" and "ay" that match the riddles.

play	day	jay	paint	tray	tail
	snail	say	pay	nail	

1. I carry my house on my back.

   _____

2. I have 24 hours.

   _____

3. I hold things together when you are building.

   _____

4. I am a blue bird.

   _____

5. You can carry things on me.

   _____

6. I make colourful pictures.

   _____

7. I am found at the back of a dog.

   _____

8. You must do this if you want to buy something.

   _____

9. This is what you do when you speak.

   _____

10. You like to do this with your friends.

   _____

Word Order: Making Sentences

C. Rewrite the following groups of words to make sentences.

1. start autumn. We in school

   _____

2. home. close My is to school

   _____

3. to I from day. every walk and school

   _____

4. lunch. go I Sometimes, home for

   _____

5. sports at There school. of are lots my

   _____

6. volleyball. and soccer, play We hockey,

   _____

7. floor I games. to like play

   _____

Word Search

D. Find the words below in the word search.

snail   may   tray   nail   trail   day
clay   say   hail   play   sail   pray

q	w	f	s	w	h	o	f	x	f	h	k	t
h	b	k	n	e	b	k	r	b	h	l	g	r
r	o	x	a	l	m	n	o	k	l	w	z	a
p	k	f	i	q	a	g	z	l	z	s	n	i
q	g	c	l	a	y	o	c	z	n	a	i	l
r	o	e	q	c	d	k	d	r	f	y	j	h
b	h	q	t	e	l	f	e	s	w	e	h	f
q	x	o	r	v	b	p	r	a	y	r	l	n
z	d	r	a	f	w	f	w	d	n	p	q	l
p	l	a	y	w	o	x	o	r	s	t	i	s
s	t	x	x	h	e	d	x	h	x	a	x	h
g	d	h	b	o	l	k	b	c	h	r	i	m
r	a	o	f	r	b	s	l	e	t	s	g	l
h	y	m	l	x	m	l	b	x	n	a	y	b

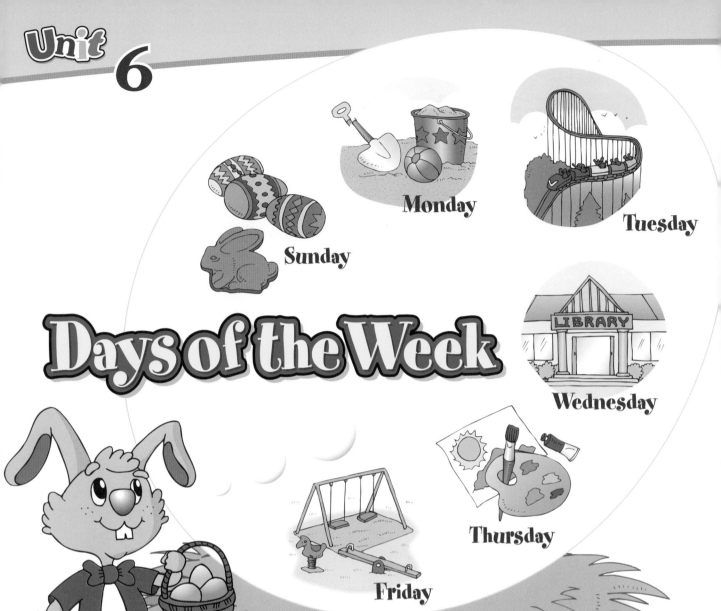

Days of the Week

Sunday

Monday

Tuesday

Wednesday

Thursday

Friday

A. Ben the Bunny has a special week ahead. Can you guess what will happen on each day? Finish the sentences.

1. On Sunday, it will be Easter.

2. On Monday, Ben _____

3. On Tuesday, _____

4. On Wednesday, _____

5. On Thursday, _____

6. On Friday, _____

7. Draw a picture of something you think Ben would like to do on Saturday and complete the sentence.

On Saturday, _____

_____

_____

_____

_____

Saturday

 Phonics: Vowel Digraphs – ea and ee

B. Underline the correct word that fits each sentence.

1. The bee   beat makes its home in a hive.

2. The blue jeans   beans are hanging on the line.

3. It's nice to have a cup of tea   tee .

4. The baseball teem   team plays in summer.

5. The bean   been plant grew very high.

6. We will have some meat   meet for dinner.

7. Mom is going to weed   week the garden.

8. There are seven days in a weak   week .

9. We sail our boat on the sea   see .

10. This seed   seek will grow into a plant.

Unit 6

Telling (Declarative) Sentences

- A **Telling Sentence** tells you something. It begins with a capital and ends with a period.

   Example: Bees get nectar from flowers.

C. Colour the picture and write four sentences about what you see.

1. _____

   _____

   _____

2. _____

   _____

   _____

3. _____

   _____

   _____

4. _____

   _____

   _____

   _____

Unscrambling Words

D. **Unscramble the words and write them in the correct order on the lines.**

ⓅⓅ

ptmeSereb   yaM   udseTay   raaJuny   yJlu

cmbeDeer   ydaFir   suAutg   eJnu   sneWdeyda

cObreto   nSdyua   yeFbuarr   odyaMn   crhaM

shTuyard   vmNeorbe   udraStya   lArpi

Months of the Year

_____

_____

_____

_____

_____

_____

_____

_____

_____

_____

_____

_____

The days of the week and months of the year begin with a capital letter.

Days of the Week

_____

_____

_____

_____

_____

_____

_____

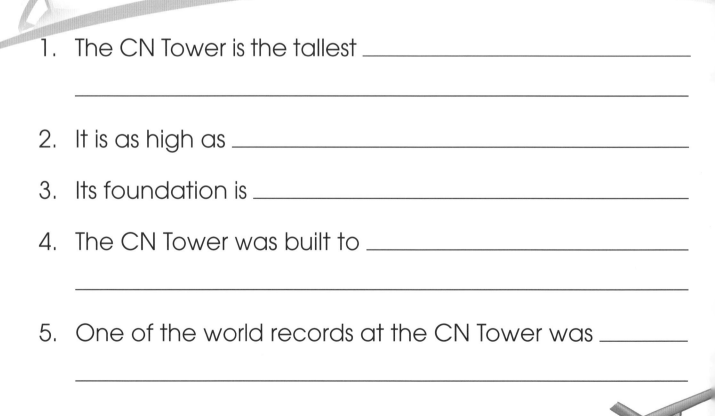

The CN (Canadian National) Tower in Toronto, Canada is the tallest self-supporting tower in the world. It is as high as five and a half football fields and has a foundation that is as deep as a five-storey building.

The CN Tower was built to improve the broadcasting of radio and television signals. Many people have used it to break world records, like the person who hopped down its 1,967 steps on a pogo stick.

THE CN Tower

A. Read the story. Finish the sentences.

1. The CN Tower is the tallest _____

_____

2. It is as high as _____

3. Its foundation is _____

4. The CN Tower was built to _____

_____

5. One of the world records at the CN Tower was _____

_____

_____

Phonics: Consonant Blends – bl, cl, fl, gl, pl, and sl

B. Write the missing consonant blends in the blanks.

bl	cl	fl	gl	pl	sl

1. Robert picked _____owers from the garden.

2. Michael saw the _____owns at the circus.

3. The children played on the _____ide.

4. His new car is _____ack.

5. The _____ass broke into many pieces.

6. They took the _____ed out in the winter.

7. There is a Canadian _____ag in front of our school.

8. Clare _____ew out the candles on the cake.

9. Maggie put the cookies on the _____ate.

10. They were _____ad they took their time.

11. The _____ock in the hall struck midnight.

12. At recess, we _____ay outside.

Asking (Interrogative) Sentences

- An **Asking sentence** asks a question.

- It begins with a capital letter and ends with a question mark (?).
  Example: What does your spaceship look like?

C. Albert the Alien has just arrived on Earth. If you could ask him five questions, what would they be?

1. _____

   _____

   _____

2. _____

   _____

3. _____

   _____

4. _____

   _____

5. _____

   _____

Ask a friend to pretend that he or she is Albert and answer your questions.

 **Identifying Polygons**

A polygon is a shape with 3 or more sides.

D. **In each case, draw the shape that matches the description.**

1. A polygon with 3 sides

2. A polygon with 4 sides

3. A polygon with 6 sides

4. A polygon with 7 sides

5. A polygon with 5 sides

6. A polygon with 8 sides

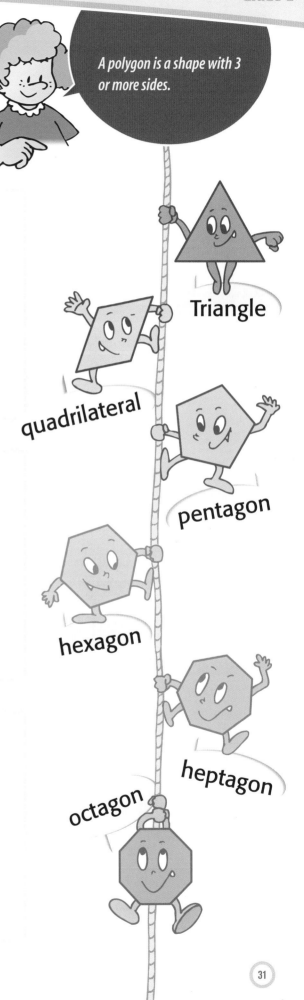

Triangle

quadrilateral

pentagon

hexagon

heptagon

octagon

Sir John A. Macdonald

The first prime minister of Canada was Sir John A. Macdonald. He was born in Glasgow, Scotland and came to Kingston, Ontario in 1816 at the age of five. He became a lawyer in 1836.

In 1867, the Dominion of Canada was formed with Sir John A. as its head. He was best known for his part in the completion of the Pacific Railway. He died in 1881 in Ottawa, the nation's capital.

A. Read the story and answer the questions.

1. Who was the first prime minister of Canada?

   _____

2. Where was he born?

   _____

3. How old was he when he came to Ontario?

   _____

4. What year was the Dominion of Canada formed?

   _____

5. What was Sir John A. best known for?

   _____

Phonics: Consonant Blends – br, cr, dr, fr, gr, pr, and tr

B. Choose the consonant blends on the bricks below to fill in the blanks.

br   **cr**   **dr**   **fr**   **gr**   **pr**   **tr**

_____ une   _____ ime   _____ op

_____ ip   _____ ape   _____ ing

_____ eam   _____ uit   _____ aid

_____ ass   _____ one   _____ ize

_____ ap   _____ ee   _____ og

_____ um   _____ ess   _____ uck

_____ ab   _____ ail   _____ ue

_____ oom   _____ eed   _____ ame

_____ een   _____ ime   _____ oss

_____ ee   _____ ail   _____ oom

Exclamatory Sentences

- Wow! An **Exclamatory Sentence** is a sentence that shows strong feeling.
- It begins with a capital letter and ends with an exclamation mark (!).

C. Change the sentences to exclamations.

1. You found a $10 bill on the ground.

    _____

2. You learned to ride a two-wheeler.

    _____

3. You have just read your first book.

    _____

4. You just learned to swim.

    _____

5. You have a new puppy.

    _____

6. You won the 1st prize.

    _____

7. You are going to Disney World.

    _____

Ordinal Numbers

- **Ordinal Numbers** *are words that state the order of people or things.*

D. Look at the pictures and their ordinal numbers. Complete the sentences below.

first

second

third

fourth

fifth

sixth

seventh

eighth

ninth

tenth

1. The football is _____ .

2. The golf ball is _____ .

3. The baseball is _____ .

4. The volleyball is _____ .

5. The tennis ball is _____ .

6. The basketball is _____ .

7. The beachball is _____ .

8. The shuttlecock is _____ .

9. The hockey puck is _____ .

10. The ping pong ball is _____ .

Dance Lessons

dance   ten
jive   fun
good   day
many
slippers   ballet
costumes

A. Read the story. Choose the words that fit in the blanks.

When Kathleen was three years old, she started to learn 1._____ . She wore a pink leotard and tiny ballet 2._____ . She practised the steps every 3._____ .

By the time she was 4._____ years old, she was very good at ballet. She learned 5._____ new steps and routines. In no time at all, she was very 6._____ at jazz, too!

Later, when Kathleen was eighteen, she saw a 7._____ competition on television. She liked the dancers and the 8._____ , too. The people were the same age as she and they were having 9._____ . Now, Kathleen is learning the 10._____ .

Phonics: Consonant Blends – sk, sm, sn, sp, st, and sw

B. Circle the correct consonant blends.

1. Yum! That meat really   st   sm   ells good!

2. There are many galaxies in outer   sk   sp   ace.

3. There are two sets of   sw   st   airs in our house.

4. Mom cooked dinner on the   st   sn   ove.

5. Oh, no! There's a   st   sk   unk by the tree.

6. The   sm   sn   ake slithered in the grass.

7. What is your   sm   sn   ack for recess?

8. We will go for a   sw   sp   im.

9. She can   sp   sk   ip with a rope.

10. The   st   sm   all child was shy.

11. Kathleen tried to   sk   sw   at the fly.

12. She tried to   sp   sn   ip the thread with the scissors.

13. Can you   sm   sn   ap your fingers?

14. I set the table with a fork, a knife, and a   sm   sp   oon.

 Imperative (Command) Sentences

• A **Command** is a sentence that tells someone to do something.

C. Robert is teaching his dog, Punkie, to obey commands. Unscramble the words to write the commands.

1. bone , the Punkie . Fetch

_____

_____

2. newspaper . and Punkie , get the go

_____

_____

3. shoe . Find Punkie , the

_____

_____

4. mouth . leash Take in the your

_____

_____

5. toy . the Find

_____

_____

6. chase Don't the car .

_____

_____

Riddles

D. Help Sunny solve the riddles below.

Toonies, Loonies, and Such

penny	nickel	dime	quarter	loonie	toonie

1. I am worth 1¢.
    I am smaller than a nickel
    but bigger than a dime.
    I have maple leaves.

    _____

2. I am worth $2.00.
    I am silver and gold.
    I am the largest coin.

    _____

3. I am worth 10¢.
    I am the smallest coin.
    I have a schooner called
    the Bluenose.

    _____

4. I am worth 25¢.
    I am larger than a nickel but
    smaller than a loonie.
    I have a caribou.

    _____

5. I am worth $1.00.
    I am golden.
    I have a loon on the front.

    _____

6. I am worth 5¢.
    I am silver.
    I am larger than a dime but
    smaller than a quarter.

    _____

Word Families

Change one letter.

A. Read the word at the beinning of each group. Read the sentences. Fill in rhyming words that make sense.

1. road   – They drove down the _____ .

              – The _____ and the frog are friends.

              – He lifted the _____ of bricks.

2. like   – I _____ to eat at McDonald's.

              – Mary rode her _____ to the store.

              – Dad and I went for a _____ .

              – _____ is a kind of fish.

3. game – We played a _____ of chess.

              – She _____ to my birthday party.

              – The baby lion is very _____ .

              – Her _____ is Judy.

4. bake   – She will _____ some cookies for us.

              – Will you _____ your umbrella today?

              – The _____ is delicious.

              – The _____ is clear and blue.

              – Mom told David to _____ the lawn.

5. day   – It is a beautiful _____ .

         – _____ is a type of bird.

         – The first _____ of sunshine beat down.

         – Did she _____ where she was going?

         – They found their _____ home.

         – Her birthday is in the month of _____ .

Beginning, Middle, and Ending Consonants

B. Fill in the missing consonants.

__ ase ①

d __ um ②

__ u __ ③

__ in ④

__ es __ ⑤

__ ate ⑥

__ o __ ⑦

__ ea __ ⑧

__ a __ ⑨

__ ar __ ⑩

__ a __ ⑪

__ oc __ ⑫

__ e __ ⑬

__ i __ ⑭

__ a __ ⑮

Short and Long Vowels

C. David loves baseball. Help him reach home base by filling in the missing vowels.

The Baseball Game

12. h ___ nd

11. f ___ ve

10. r ___ ke

9. c ___ be

3rd

1. t ___ be

8. f ___ sh

2. c ___ ke

7. t ___ nt

1st

2nd

3. l ___ g

4. b ___ ne

5. p ___ le

6. h ___ ve

Vowel Digraphs and Consonant Blends

D. Find the words listed below in the word search.

flag	tray	blue	reed	fruit	pail
slide	weed	cream	play	plate	snake
dream	tree	glass	clock	bean	stove
week	prize	grass	broom	tail	been

y	l	w	g	w	t	r	a	y	q	x	p	z	p	z	s
x	w	e	k	x	a	h	i	x	p	d	w	f	e	k	d
f	h	h	i	c	i	x	t	a	b	k	o	p	r	i	b
l	t	p	a	i	l	k	e	f	c	x	c	l	o	c	k
a	w	l	o	z	s	i	v	r	i	u	o	a	v	d	c
g	l	a	s	s	t	h	t	o	d	s	r	t	f	m	i
z	t	y	m	o	o	d	u	w	b	l	u	e	m	i	x
p	y	x	s	t	v	o	j	m	e	i	n	f	c	k	b
s	n	a	k	e	e	n	r	o	e	d	e	j	n	b	r
p	w	o	o	r	x	b	e	a	n	e	k	a	i	a	o
o	c	w	f	x	i	c	e	q	x	j	q	u	w	q	o
o	j	s	p	w	e	e	d	y	u	w	y	w	e	u	m
n	b	z	i	e	h	l	k	o	i	a	f	h	q	a	c
v	l	d	r	e	a	m	s	r	x	l	r	l	c	b	o
e	v	s	w	k	t	h	t	s	h	v	u	t	r	e	e
w	h	z	d	w	c	x	j	b	p	r	i	z	e	x	g
o	j	o	w	g	p	e	z	i	g	x	t	g	a	g	o
g	r	a	s	s	x	v	h	q	c	o	s	z	m	d	x

Sentences

E. Give each sentence a correct punctuation and circle "T" for telling, "A" for asking, "E" for exclamatory, and "I" for imperative.

1.	Kate loves chocolate cake	T	A	E	I
2.	Will David sweep the floor	T	A	E	I
3.	They shop at the mall	T	A	E	I
4.	Open the door	T	A	E	I
5.	Do you like ice cream	T	A	E	I
6.	Oh, no	T	A	E	I
7.	Don't talk to strangers	T	A	E	I
8.	I won the first prize	T	A	E	I

F. Underline the nouns and circle the verbs.

1. The car drove down the highway.

2. The bird laid the eggs in the nest.

3. Mom bakes great cakes at home.

4. Tom walks to school every day.

5. She likes to take the dog for a walk.

Subject / Predicate Match-up

The subject tells whom or what the sentence is about. The predicate tells what the subject is doing.

G. Match the subjects with the predicates by writing the letters in the boxes.

1. The clown ☐   A. came down from the sky.

2. Dad ☐   B. wore face make-up.

3. A train ☐   C. chugged along the tracks.

4. Five frogs ☐   D. jumped on the lily pad.

5. My school ☐   E. has a big gymnasium.

6. Leaves ☐   F. often turn colours in Autumn.

7. A comet ☐   G. gave me a big hug.

H. For each sentence, fill in a subject and a predicate.

1. The _____ _____ to the beach.

2. An _____ _____ a fruit.

3. Many _____ _____ to the farm daily.

4. Every _____ , we _____ to the lunchroom.

5. Each _____ , they _____ skiing.

6. A _____ _____ a vehicle.

The Treasure Chest

Dear Dave,

We went to Sharaz last Thursday. When we arrived, we heard about a sunken ship in the shallow sea. The story goes like this – a pirate ship sank there long ago and there are still treasure chests aboard.

We decided to search for the sunken treasure. First, we boarded a small boat and rowed out to the ship. Then, we put on wetsuits and masks and dived under the water.

When we reached the ship, we swam inside and, guess what? We found a giant chest filled with gold and jewels!

I'll send you some photos as soon as I get them.

Your friend,
Rob

A. Read the letter and answer the questions.

1. What is the main idea of the first paragraph?

   _____

   _____

2. What is the main idea of the second paragraph?

   _____

   _____

Phonics: **Consonant Digraphs – ch, sh, th, and wh**

B. Fill in the missing letters to make the tongue twisters.

Tongue twisters with ch, sh, th, and wh are sometimes hard to say.

Ch 1. _____ ester _____ ewed the _____ ewing gum _____ eerily.

Sh 2. _____ e sells sea _____ ells by the sea _____ ore.

Th 3. _____ addeus _____ ought _____ e _____ imble was _____ ick.

Wh 4. Willy the _____ ale _____ irled _____ ile the _____ eel of the _____ ite _____ aler _____ istled.

C. In each case, choose the word that fits.

1. A cat's _____ help her find her way. (whisper, whiskers)

2. This gravy is _____ . (thick, think)

3. The _____ sank in the sea. (ship, shop)

4. The treasure _____ was filled with jewels. (cheat, chest)

5. _____ is a delicious fruit. (Beach, Peach)

6. A _____ flies toward light. (moth, math)

Unit 10

 Common Nouns

- A **Common Noun** names any person, place, or thing.
- It can be singular (one) or plural (more than one).

D. Add "s" to write the plural form of the singular nouns.

1. dog _____

2. mat _____

3. acorn _____

4. desk _____

5. ship _____

6. table _____

7. fox _____

8. girl _____

9. ruler _____

10. lake _____

11. boat _____

12. road _____

13. toy _____

14. tree _____

15. flower _____

16. plant _____

17. rug _____

18. flag _____

19. boy _____

20. mask _____

Baby Animals

E.   Read the sentences. Look at the pictures and fill in the blanks.

| deer   dog   horse   goose   cat   pig |
| chicken   rabbit   cow   kangaroo |

1.   A foal is a baby _____ .

2.   A calf is a baby _____ .

3.   A leveret is a baby _____ .

4.   A puppy is a baby _____ .

5.   A joey is a baby _____ .

6.   A piglet is a baby _____ .

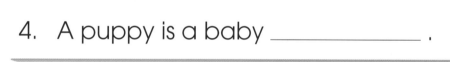

7.   A chick is a baby _____ .

8.   A gosling is a baby _____ .

9.   A kitten is a baby _____ .

10.   A fawn is a baby _____ .

Unit 11

A Visit to the Farm

There are many different kinds of farms. Some are dairy farms and some are cattle farms. There are others that grow vegetables, like corn, potatoes, and carrots. In the West, farmers grow wheat.

Our class visited a farm. It was a dairy farm, so the animals were all cows. The farmer showed us how the cows are milked using big machines.

We had lots of fun at the farm.

A. Answer the questions.

1. What is the main idea of the story?

   _____

2. What kind of farm did the children visit?

   _____

3. What did the farmer use to milk the cows?

   _____

Phonics: R-controlled Vowels

- *When the letter "r" follows a vowel, it changes the sound of the vowel.*

B. **Arnie the Farmer is going to the market. Help him get there. Underline the correct words.**

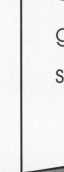

Arnie
Farm

Arnie's (form, farm) is (for, far) from the (market, marked). Every day, Arnie (works, worms) very (hard, harm). He (turms, turns) the soil, which is sometimes called (dirt, diet). When there are lots of (warms, worms) in the soil, it is healthy. There are also lots of animals on the (form, farm). Some are (horns, horses) and others are pigs, from which Arnie gets (park, pork) to sell at the market.

Proper Nouns

- A **Proper Noun** names a specific person, place, or thing.
- It always begins with a capital letter.

C. Colour the pages of the books that contain proper nouns.

1. boy | Mark

2. Ottawa | city

3. Venus | planet

4. Mrs. Smith | mother

5. Sun | star

6. dog | Punkie

7. Portland Drive | street

8. Mars | chocolate bar

9. Canada Day | holiday

10. day | Sunday

11. The Gap | store

12. Charlotte's Web | book

13. Deer Lake | town

14. month | May

Countries and Languages

D. Fill in the blanks.

Country	Language
Spain	Spanish
Italy	Italian
France	French
Greece	Greek
Canada	English
Romania	Romanian
Hungary	Hungarian

Many countries in the world have people who speak 1._____ , such as Canada. In Spain, people speak 2._____ and in 3._____ , people speak French. In the Eastern European countries of Hungary and Romania, people speak 4._____ and 5._____ . In Italy and Greece, people speak 6._____ and 7._____ .

E. Unscramble these languages.

LIAANTI
1
_____

HASPNSI
2
_____

GRHUAIANN
3
_____

Out on the Road

A. Time to Nibble
B. Home Sweet Home
C. Time for a Drink
D. Derek Turns the Curve
E. On the Straight and Narrow
F. Derek Hits the Fence

A. Derek the Dog is out on the road. Help him find his way home. Match the story titles below with the pictures in the maze. Print the letters in the boxes.

1

2

3

4

5

6

Phonics: Dipthongs – ou and ow

- **Dipthongs** are two vowels that make a new sound.

B. Say the words in the clouds below and print them where they belong.

hound   grow   blow   row   blouse

couch   glow   town   brown   rainbow

mouse   low   flowers   crown   sound

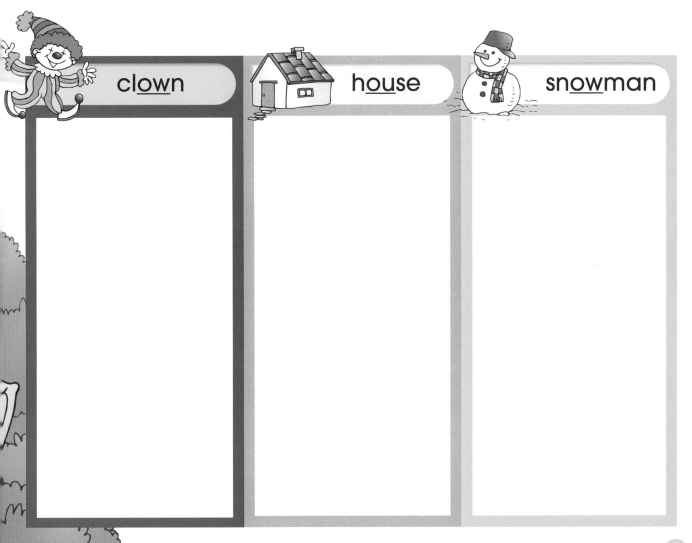

clown   house   snowman

Plural Nouns

C. **Look at the picture. Find the objects listed below. Count them and write the number words with the plural nouns.**

streetlight		car	
flower		boy	
bicycle		tree	
parking meter		truck	

Homonyms

- **Homonyms** are word pairs that sound the same but have different meanings and are spelled differently.

D. Match the pictures and words with the homonyms.

1.  pear ☐

2.  sew ☐

3. 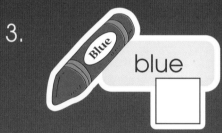 blue ☐

4.  sun ☐

5.  see ☐

6.  toe ☐

7.  flower ☐

8.  witch ☐

 A. sea    B. blew    C. flour   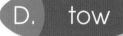 D. tow

E. which   F. so   G. pair   H. son

The Coin Collection

David has a coin collection. He started it when he was six years old. He has over three hundred coins in his collection.

The first coins he got were three coins from Italy that his mom gave him after a trip there. Since then, many of his family members and friends have given him coins for gifts. He has coins from all over the world.

David's favourite coin is one from Sri Lanka. It is large and heavy. Another coin he likes is a Chinese one with a hole in the centre.

A. Read the story. Finish the sentences.

1. David has a _____

2. He has over _____

3. His first coins were _____

4. Many people have given _____

5. He has coins from _____

6. David's favourite _____

7. His favourite coin is _____

8. A Chinese coin has _____

Phonics: Dipthongs – oi and oy

- *"Oi" and "oy" sound the same in words, but "oi" is usually found in the middle of a word and "oy" is usually found at the end.*

B. Read the sentences below. Fill in the blanks with words from the word bank.

coin	toy	annoy	soy	oil
boy	joy	boil	point	loyal

1. Marie is a very _____ friend.

2. Christine has a _____ collection.

3. The _____ likes to play soccer.

4. Ryan gets a lot of _____ from playing sports.

5. The pencil has a very sharp _____ .

6. Some babies drink _____ milk.

7. Don't _____ your brother!

8. Will you _____ the water for tea?

9. The Game Boy is his favourite _____ .

10. _____ is lighter than water.

Unit 13

Verbs (Action Words)

- **Verbs** are words that describe actions.

  Example: running – She is running a race.

C. **Find these actions in the picture and write a sentence using each one.**

swinging	playing	running	climbing	sliding

1. _____

2. _____

3. _____

4. _____

5. _____

Synonyms

- **Synonyms** *are words that mean the same thing.*

D. Read each sentence below. Circle the word that matches the one underlined.

1. Cindy was <u>weeping</u> when she fell down.

   crying   climbing

2. It was a <u>windy</u> day in the city.

   breezy   cool

3. Mom was <u>exhausted</u> after her trip.

   tired   trying

4. The <u>small</u> child held on to the balloon.

   little   large

5. The weather was <u>humid</u> and warm.

   damp   dry

6. The <u>huge</u> dog ran over to the car.   big   tiny

7. The kiwi fruit were <u>firm</u> and green.   hard   soft

8. The bike tires were <u>grimy</u> after they went through the mud.

   dirty   wet

1. Turn the oven up to 400° F.

2. Get these ingredients together.
   2 cups of flour
   1/2 cup of sugar
   1/2 cup of margarine (melted)
   1/2 tsp. of salt
   3 tsp. of baking powder
   1 cup of blueberries
   1 egg
   3/4 cup of milk

3. Put all the dry ingredients in a bowl.

4. Put all the wet ingredients in a bowl.

5. Mix the dry ingredients with the wet ingredients.

6. Spoon the mixture into a muffin pan.

7. Bake at 400° F for 15 – 20 minutes.

Making Blueberry Muffins

A. Read the cookbook recipe above. Circle the correct answers.

1. This recipe is for (muffins, cookies).

2. Milk is a (wet, dry) ingredient.

3. The fruit in this recipe is (blackberries, blueberries).

4. The seventh ingredient is (egg, milk).

5. The oven is turned up to (400°F, 400°C).

Phonics: Special Sound "oo"

- Words that have "**oo**" in them can sound like "oo" in "room" or "oo" in "cook".

B.   Complete the rhymes with the words provided.

cookbook   cook   book   look

My mom taught me to 1._____

By reading a 2._____ .

She said, " Take a 3._____ .

This is called a 4._____ . "

fool   pool   drool

cool

The clown played the 5._____

Jumping in the 6._____ .

He thought it was 7._____

When he started to 8._____ .

Unit 14

"Being" Verbs (am, is, are)

- "**Am**", "**is**", and "**are**" are special verbs that tell about someone or something.

  Rules: Use "am" with "I".

  Use "is" when it's one person, place, or thing.

  Use "are" when it's more than one person, place, or thing.

C.   Fill "am", "is", or "are" in the blanks.

1. Jason _____ riding his bike.

2. Kathleen and David _____ flying a kite.

3. She _____ planning to see the circus.

4. Maria _____ running to the bus.

5. There _____ three boys in the play.

6. They _____ best friends.

7. We _____ looking for the soccer ball.

8. I _____ going to the show with my dad.

9. Rob _____ driving his car.

10. It _____ a nice morning.

Antonyms

- **Antonyms** are words with opposite meanings.

D. Read the word inside each kite. Choose the correct antonym from the two words below it.

1 hot — warm, cold

2 tall — short, high

3 fat — heavy, thin

4 dry — heat, wet

5 happy — funny, sad

6 sick — healthy, ill

7 black — green, white

8 afraid — brave, scared

9 ask — question, answer

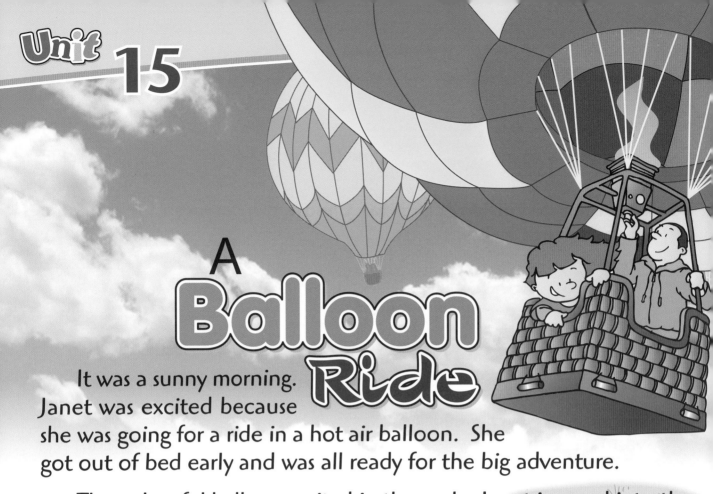

A Balloon Ride

It was a sunny morning. Janet was excited because she was going for a ride in a hot air balloon. She got out of bed early and was all ready for the big adventure.

The colourful balloon waited in the park. Janet jumped into the basket. She was ready to fly. The man in the basket used a burner to make the air hot. The balloon began to lift off slowly. Up they went into the sky. Janet felt like a bird flying over the tops of the trees and houses.

A. Circle "T" for true or "F" for false to each sentence. If it is false, write the correct sentence on the line below.

1. It was a sunny afternoon.

   _____ T F

2. The balloon was colourful.

   _____ T F

3. The balloon was in the schoolyard.

   _____ T F

4. The balloon lifted off quickly.

   _____ T F

Phonics: **Silent Consonants**

- Some words have **Silent Consonants**. We don't hear the sound of the consonant when we say the word.
  Example: Don't clim<u>b</u> up the tree.

B. Sometimes an "l" is silent. Add the silent "l" and say the words.

1. ha [ ] f

2. ta [ ] k

3. sta [ ] k

4. wa [ ] k

5. ca [ ] f

6. pa [ ] m

C. Answer the riddles with the silent "b" words.

(lamb)   (limb)   (thumb)   (crumb)

1. This is a young sheep.   _____

2. You should keep this on your plate.   _____

3. The finger that is nearest your wrist.   _____

4. It is something found on some animals.   _____

 **Subject: Verb**

- *The subject of a sentence must have a verb that "agrees".*

D. Read the facts about beavers. Choose the verb that agrees with the subject in each sentence.

1. Beavers _____ members of the aquatic rodent family.   is   are

2. Every beaver _____ a coat of thick coarse fur.   have   has

3. Beavers _____ their dams with sticks and mud in streams and small rivers.   build   builds

4. Beavers _____ in colonies, with one or more groups to a lodge.   live   lives

5. A family of beavers _____ of a mother, father, and two sets of offspring.   consist   consists

6. They _____ in the winter.   breed   breeds

Antonyms

Antonyms are words with opposite meanings.

E. **Find the antonyms in each sentence and write them on the lines below.**

1. The hot air balloon needs cold air to land.

   _____ _____

2. Janet woke up early so that she would not be late for the balloon ride.

   _____ _____

3. The best time to fly a balloon is on a calm day and the worst time is on a windy day.

   _____ _____   _____ _____

4. Janet opened her eyes when the balloon went up but she closed them when it came down.

   _____ _____   _____ _____

It isn't really that easy.

F. **Write a sentence using the antonyms "easy" and "hard".**

Unit 16

Autumn

carpet   beautiful   season
fall   fawns   Summer
woods   because
colour   hike   animals
woods   ground

A. Read the words above. Find the spaces where they belong in the story.

Autumn is the 1._____ that follows 2._____ . Sometimes, we call it 3._____ . It is very 4._____ 5._____ the leaves change 6._____ and fall to the 7._____ . When they fall, the ground looks like a 8._____ .

It is fun to 9._____ in autumn. Often, there are lots of 10._____ in the 11._____ in autumn. Baby deer or 12._____ can be seen even in 13._____ near cities.

B. Answer the questions on the lines below.

1. What season follows summer?

_____

2. What happens to leaves in autumn?

_____

3. Where do you find baby deer in autumn?

_____

4. What is another name for autumn?

_____

5. What season comes after autumn?

_____

Phonics: "Sad" Sounds – au and aw

- Both "**au**" and "**aw**" make the **Sad Sound**. When you say "saw" or "pause" out loud, you can hear why these are sad sounds.

C. Answer the questions with the correct words from the box.

jaw	autumn	yawn	auto
fawn	straw	saw	saucer

I saw a fawn open its jaws and yawn!

1. What is a baby deer? _____

2. What is part of your face? _____

3. What do you put in a drink? _____

4. What is another word for car? _____

5. What can be used to cut wood? _____

6. What season is also called "fall"? _____

7. What goes on the bottom of a cup? _____

8. What do you do when you are sleepy? _____

 Adjectives

- An **Adjective** is a word that describes a person, place, or thing.
  Example: The <u>little</u> girl is wearing a <u>new</u> dress.

D. **Underline the two adjectives in each sentence.**

1. The tired boys rested under the shady tree.

2. He put a big book into a small bag.

3. The friendly nurse is helping the sick girl.

4. The old man is talking to the young child.

5. She picked a red apple from the tall tree.

6. The black puppy is playing with a red ball.

E. **Use each pair of adjectives to make a sentence.**

1. small and round
2. soft and fluffy
3. bright and colourful
4. long and thin

1. _____

2. _____

3. _____

4. _____

Homonyms, Synonyms, and Antonyms

F. Read the pair of words in each leaf. Decide if they are synonyms (S), homonyms (H), or antonyms (A). Circle the correct letter.

> Homonyms are words that sound the same. Synonyms are words that have similar meaning. Antonyms are words with opposite meanings.

1.

breezy
windy

S
H
A

2.

pair
pear

S
H
A

3.

little
big

S
H
A

4.

close
open

S
H
A

5.

sad
unhappy

S
H
A

6.

hairy
bald

S
H
A

7.

night
day

S
H
A

8.

clean
dirty

S
H
A

9.

blue
blew

S
H
A

Most plants start as a seed. Usually, you plant the seed in the garden or the yard, in shade or sun.

If you use a small trowel, you can dig a hole just big enough to poke the seed down and cover it with more soil.

First, you plant the seed and let the sun shine down on it. After a few weeks, little shoots begin to sprout. Then, the stem gets stronger and leaves begin to show.

All about
Plants

A. Answer the questions.

1. What do most plants start as?

   _____

2. Where do people usually plant the seeds?

   _____

3. What do people use to cover a seed?

   _____

4. How long does it take for shoots to sprout?

   _____

Phonics: Words with "y" as a Vowel

- Sometimes when "**y**" is at the end of a word, it sounds like an "e".
  Examples: many, only, penny

B. Say the words on the left. Match them with the meanings.

funny	another name for rabbit
honey	causing laughter
money	bright with sunshine
Mary	a sweet, sticky fluid made by bees
bunny	a name for a girl
sunny	used for buying and selling things

C. Fill in the missing words.

my   try   Why   fly   shy

Sometimes, the "y" at the end of a word sounds like an "i".

1. _____ did she go to the store?

2. Did you _____ to ride the bike?

3. We can _____ our kites another day.

4. The child was very _____ .

5. We can go to _____ house to play.

 Past Tense Verbs

- Some verbs tell what happened in the past. You can add "**ed**" to them.

D. Add "ed" to the clue words and complete the crossword puzzle.

Across

A. plant
B. want
C. train
D. end
E. learn

Down

1. treat
2. sail
3. play
4. answer
5. need

Months of the Year

E.   Read the sentences below. Fill in the correct months.

October   July   January   June
November   April   December   February
March   May   August   September

1.   In _____ , it is Christmas.

2.   School starts in _____ .

3.   Valentine's Day falls in _____ .

4.   Halloween is at the end of _____ .

5.   The first month of the year is _____ .

6.   The month in which school ends for the summer vacation is _____ .

7.   The eighth month of the year is _____ .

8.   The second last month of the year is _____ .

9.   St. Patrick's Day is in _____ .

10.   This month rhymes with "day". _____

11.   Canada Day is in this month. _____

Penguins

Penguins are birds that cannot fly but are good swimmers. They live in Antarctica and off the coasts of Africa and Australia. The smallest penguin is 40 cm tall. It is called the Blue Fairy. The tallest penguin is the Emperor. It can be 120 cm tall.

Penguins feed on fish, squid, and small shrimp. They are the prey of leopard seals and killer whales. The female penguin lays an egg or two and goes off in search of food. While she is gone, the male hatches the eggs on his feet under a layer of fur.

A. Read the story. Write the correct answers in the blanks.

1. Penguins live in _____ and off the coasts of _____ and _____ .

2. The smallest penguin is called the _____ .

3. It is _____ tall.

4. The tallest penguin is called the _____ .

5. Penguins feed on _____ , _____ , and _____ .

6. The _____ lays eggs and the _____ hatches them.

Phonics: Soft and Hard "c" and "g"

- The letters "**c**" and "**g**" have both **Soft** and **Hard Sounds**.
  Examples: celery (soft "c" sound); can (hard "c" sound)
  ginger (soft "g" sound); go (hard "g" sound)

B. Read the words and place them in the correct ice floes below.

giant create cake gate clown gym grow
city giraffe cent
gem circus goose cook girl

SOFT c

HARD c

SOFT g

HARD g

Irregular Past Tense Verbs

- Some verbs don't end in "ed".
  Examples: sing ➡ sang; speak ➡ spoke

C. Match up the present and past tenses.

1. write • • thought
2. drink • • wrote
3. ring • • drank
4. think • • left
5. drive • • drove
6. leave • • rang

D. Write the present form of the past tense verbs in the cakes.

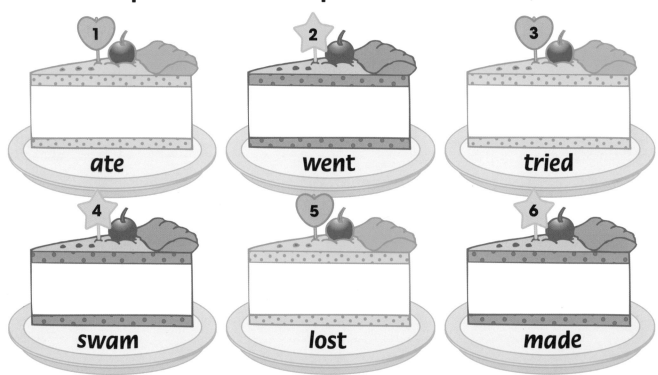

1. ate
2. went
3. tried
4. swam
5. lost
6. made

The Computer

We use computers everywhere – at school, at home, at the doctor's, the dentist's, and the department stores. It is important to know the main parts of the computer. The monitor is the screen that displays words and pictures. When you type on a keyboard, your words appear on the monitor. If you want a paper copy, you can use a printer to print the words or pictures. Some computers use diskettes to save work and others use CDs , which look the same as the ones you use to play music. If you add a modem to your computer, you can communicate with other people.

Word Search

E. Circle the words that are underlined above.

z	b	y	d	i	s	k	e	t	t	e	s
o	u	n	o	q	c	k	b	s	j	x	c
j	p	r	i	n	t	e	r	a	l	b	o
k	d	b	i	a	b	y	o	f	e	u	m
o	e	a	u	e	u	b	h	c	j	i	p
r	u	f	c	r	m	o	d	e	m	b	u
i	c	t	d	s	c	a	o	n	e	r	t
m	o	n	i	t	o	r	d	k	e	l	e
j	v	s	i	w	o	d	h	g	s	k	r

A. Fill in the blanks with the words below.

smell   plates   small
oceans   weigh
length   chew   pitches
whole   breathing

Whales live in 1._____ throughout the world. Some whales have between 2 and 300 teeth, while others have no teeth at all. The whales that have no teeth feed on 2._____ organisms and use long bristles called 3._____ to eat them. Those that have teeth do not 4._____ their prey but eat them 5._____ .

Whales range in 6._____ from 1.3 metres to almost 30 metres. They 7._____ anywhere from 45 kg to 136,000 kg. Some whales have little sense of 8._____ and some none at all. Their hearing, however, allows them to hear 9._____ much higher than what we can hear.

Small whales can hold their breath for several minutes, and larger ones stay underwater without 10._____ for many hours.

A visit to the
Hockey Hall of Fame

A common noun names any person, place, or thing. A proper noun names a specific person, place, or thing.

B. Read the story. Circle the common nouns. Underline the proper nouns.

David and his friend, Judy, are going to visit the Hockey Hall of Fame in downtown Toronto, Canada. It is in a large building not far from Union Station, where the friends are taking the subway from Mississauga to Toronto.

There are so many exciting exhibits at the Hockey Hall of Fame. There are pieces of equipment worn by famous hockey players, like Wayne Gretzky. The Stanley Cup, which is awarded to the top hockey team each year, is sometimes on display there.

The children want to see the first mask that was worn by Jacques Plante and some of the old hockey uniforms from years gone by. Maybe, if they're lucky, they might see a visiting hockey player.

The last thing David and Judy go to see is all the statistics of players who broke many records over the years. Players like Gordie Howe, Jean Beliveau, and Wayne Gretzky changed the game of hockey forever.

Using Code

C. Use the code to fill in the blanks.

A	B	C	D	E	F	G	H	I	J	K	L	M	N	O
1	2	3	4	5	6	7	8	9	10	11	12	13	14	15

P	Q	R	S	T	U	V	W	X	Y	Z
16	17	18	19	20	21	22	23	24	25	26

___ ___ ___ ___ ___ ___ is one of the
3 1 14 1 4 1

___ ___ ___ ___ ___ ___ ___ countries in the world. It is
12 1 18 7 5 19 20

one of three countries that make up

___ ___ ___ ___ ___ ___ ___ ___ ___ ___ ___ ___ . It is
14 15 18 20 8   1 13 5 18 9 3 1

made up of ___ ___ ___ provinces and
20 5 14

___ ___ ___ ___ ___ territories. ___ ___ ___ ___ ___ ___ ___
20 8 18 5 5   14 21 14 1 22 21 20

became the newest territory in 1999.

There are ___ ___ ___ ___ Atlantic provinces and
6 15 21 18

___ ___ ___ ___ ___ of them are called
20 8 18 5 5

___ ___ ___ ___ ___ ___ ___ ___ provinces.
13 1 18 9 20 9 13 5

There are also ___ ___ ___ ___ ___ Prairie provinces.
20 8 18 5 5

Grammar Focus

D. Circle the correct answers.

1. Maria is / are from the Philippines.

2. Frank and I like / likes to watch football.

3. David play / plays his guitar every day.

4. Kathleen studied / studyed hard before her exams.

5. May take / takes the dog for a walk daily.

6. They have / has lunch together.

7. That clown laugh / laughs loudly.

8. John is / am good at cooking.

9. Rob fix / fixed his own car.

10. I is / am hungry.

E. Make a sentence with each adjective.

1. tall

_____

2. beautiful

_____

3. friendly

_____

Vocabulary Building

Homonyms are words that sound the same but have different meanings.

F. Underline the correct homonyms.

1. sail (sale, seal)

2. see (sea, say)

3. pair (pear, peal)

4. male (mail, mane)

5. blew (blue, blow)

6. vain (vane, van)

G. Circle the synonym for each word below.

1. big (small / large)

2. weep (sweep / cry)

3. small (tiny / big)

4. dash (run / walk)

5. jump (hop / jog)

6. unhappy (sad / cheery)

Synonyms are words that have similar meanings.

H. Circle the correct antonyms.

1. dark (night / bright)

2. wet (dry / wide)

3. dirty (clean / muddy)

4. open (close / wide)

5. sad (happy / mad)

6. light (heavy / easy)

Antonyms are words that have opposite meanings.

Vowels that Sound like "e" or "i"

I.   Colour "e" or "i" to show what each word sounds like.

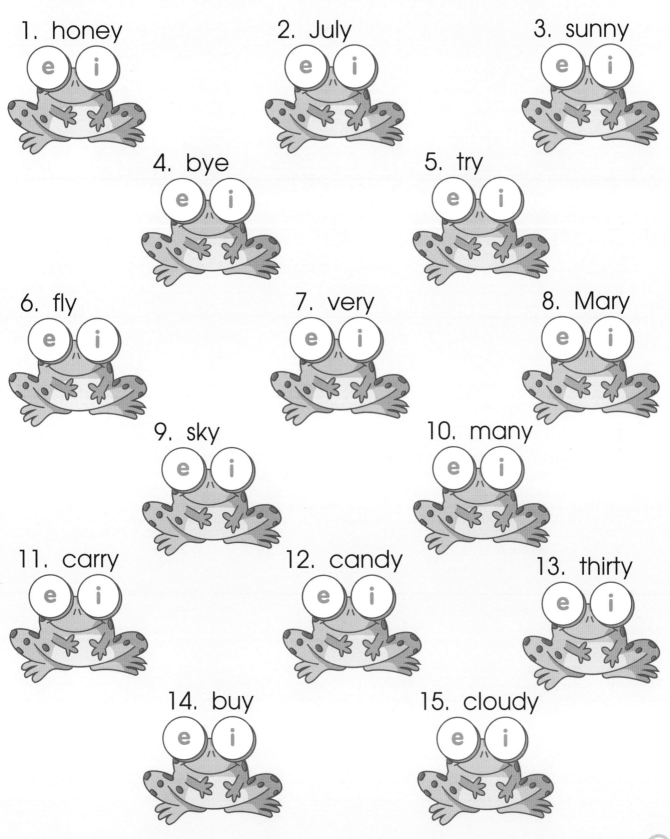

1. honey   e   i

2. July   e   i

3. sunny   e   i

4. bye   e   i

5. try   e   i

6. fly   e   i

7. very   e   i

8. Mary   e   i

9. sky   e   i

10. many   e   i

11. carry   e   i

12. candy   e   i

13. thirty   e   i

14. buy   e   i

15. cloudy   e   i

Answers

1 The Bumblebee

A. 1. It is an insect.
2. It is yellow and black.
3. The queen bee is the leader.
4. After a winter in hibernation.
B. 1. leaf   2. cap
3. bat   4. jug
5. yarn   6. wagon
7. goat   8. rabbit
9. drum   10. top
11. fan   12. queen
13. sun   14. hat
C. 1. Polar bears live in the Arctic. They are big and white. <u>Big paws.</u> They have small eyes and ears. <u>Jump from ice floe to ice floe.</u>
2. Polar bears have other names. <u>Sometimes called white bears, sea bears, or ice bears.</u> <u>Swim very well.</u>
3. Polar bears move fast and travel far. <u>Eat seals and fish.</u> The male is usually larger than the female. <u>Hairy feet.</u>
4. Baby bears or cubs are born in winter. <u>Weigh 2 pounds when born.</u> <u>Remain with mothers from 10 months to 2 years.</u>
D. 1. A square is a shape with four equal sides.
2. A triangle is a shape with three sides.
3. A circle is a single line.
4. A rectangle is a shape with opposite sides that are equal.

2 The Museum Trip

A. 1. B   2. B
3. B   4. C
B. 1. bus   2. box
3. nest   4. dime
5. tulip   6. mask
7. bar   8. pot
9. pen   10. bone
11. can   12. ball
13. sock   14. saw
15. kite   16. rake
C. 1. Apples   2. The CN Tower
3. The earth   4. A computer
5. Skating   6. The time
7. (Individual drawing and answer)
D. 1. Hockey   2. Baseball
3. Hockey ; Baseball   4. Hockey
5. Baseball   6. Hockey
7. Baseball   8. Hockey ; Baseball

3 The Eurotunnel

A. 1. England and France.
2. In 1993.
3. Napolean.
4. Two are for trains to carry people and one is for emergency and service.
B. 1. lamp   2. web
3. mop   4. jug
5. pot   6. bag
7. desk   8. bell
9. net   10. can
11. lips   12. fan
13. tent   14. rock
15. six   16. nut
C. (Individual writing)
D. 1. cup ; bowl ; glass
2. blackboard ; desk ; eraser
3. tires ; horn ; key
4. swing ; seesaw ; slide
5. pear ; grapes ; apple

4 Snakes

A. 1. reptiles   2. long
3. cold   4. eggs
5. laid   6. hibernation
7. skins   8. move
9. place
B. 1. bike   2. hive
3. pole   4. cone
5. cake   6. tube
7. kite   8. ruler
9. gate   10. tulip
C. (Order may vary.)
1. At the zoo, we visit the animals.
2. The monkey likes to hang by its tail.
3. The African elephant is the largest living land animal.
4. The zebra is black and white.
5. The male lion has a mane on its neck.
6. The tiger is orange and black.
7. The zookeeper helps clean the cages.
D. 1. recipe
2. cupboard / box
3. ingredients
4. cupboard
5. refrigerator
6. pot ; stove ; melted
7. square

Answers

5 What Happens Next?

A. (Individual writing)

B. 1. snail   2. day
   3. nail   4. jay
   5. tray   6. paint
   7. tail   8. pay
   9. say   10. play

C. 1. We start school in autumn.
   2. My school is close to home.
   3. I walk to and from school every day.
   4. Sometimes, I go home for lunch.
   5. There are lots of sports at my school.
   6. We play hockey, soccer, and volleyball. / We play soccer, hockey, and volleyball.
   7. I like to play floor games.

D.

q	w	f	s	w	h	o	f	x	f	h	k	t
h	b	k	n	e	b	k	r	b	h	l	g	r
r	o	x	a	l	m	n	o	k	l	w	z	a
p	k	f	i	q	a	g	z	l	z	s	n	i
q	g	c	l	a	y	o	c	z	n	a	i	l
r	o	e	q	c	d	k	d	r	f	y	j	h
b	h	q	t	e	l	f	e	s	w	e	h	f
q	x	o	r	v	b	p	r	a	y	r	l	n
z	d	r	a	f	w	f	w	d	n	p	q	l
p	l	a	y	w	o	x	o	r	s	t	i	s
s	t	x	x	h	e	d	x	h	x	a	x	h
g	d	h	b	o	l	k	b	c	h	r	i	m
r	a	o	f	r	b	s	l	e	t	s	g	l
h	y	m	l	x	m	l	b	x	n	a	y	b

6 Days of the Week

A. (Suggested answers)
   2. On Monday, Ben will go to the beach.
   3. On Tuesday, he will ride on the roller coaster.
   4. On Wednesday, he will go to the library.
   5. On Thursday, he will paint a picture.
   6. On Friday, he will go to the children's playground.
   7. (Individual drawing and writing)

B. 1. bee   2. jeans
   3. tea   4. team
   5. bean   6. meat
   7. weed   8. week
   9. sea   10. seed

C. (Individual colouring and writing)

D. **Months of the Year:**
   January ; February ; March ; April ; May ; June ; July ; August ; September ; October ; November ; December
   Days of the Week:
   Sunday ; Monday ; Tuesday ; Wednesday ; Thursday ; Friday ; Saturday

7 The CN Tower

A. 1. The CN Tower is the tallest self-supporting tower in the world.
   2. It is a as high as five and a half football fields.
   3. Its foundation is as deep as a five-storey building.
   4. The CN Tower was built to improve the broadcasting of radio and television signals.
   5. One of the world records at the CN Tower was a person hopping down its 1,967 steps on a pogo stick.

B. 1. flowers   2. clowns
   3. slide   4. black
   5. glass   6. sled
   7. flag   8. blew
   9. plate   10. glad
   11. clock   12. play

C. (Individual writing)

D. (Suggested drawings)

1.
2.
3.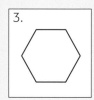
4.
5.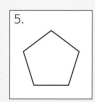
6.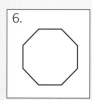

8 Sir John A. Macdonald

A. 1. Sir John A. Macdonald.
   2. Glasgow, Scotland.
   3. Five.
   4. In 1867.

5. The completion of the Pacific Railway.
B.   (Suggested answers)
prune ; prime ; crop
grip ; grape ; bring
cream ; fruit ; braid
grass ; drone ; prize
trap ; tree ; frog
drum ; dress ; truck
crab ; trail ; true
broom ; breed ; frame
green ; crime ; cross
free ; frail ; groom
C.   (Individual writing)
D. 1. the first
2. the eighth
3. the second
4. the sixth
5. the fifth
6. the fourth
7. the seventh
8. the ninth
9. the third
10. the tenth

9 Dance Lessons

A. 1. ballet
2. slippers
3. day
4. ten
5. many
6. good
7. dance
8. costumes
9. fun
10. jive
B. 1. Yum! That meat really **smells** good!
2. There are many galaxies in outer **space**.
3. There are two sets of **stairs** in our house.
4. Mom cooked dinner on the **stove**.
5. Oh, no! There's a **skunk** by the tree.
6. The **snake** slithered in the grass.
7. What is your **snack** for recess?
8. We will go for a **swim**.
9. She can **skip** with a rope.
10. The **small** child was shy.
11. Kathleen tried to **swat** the fly.
12. She tried to **snip** the thread with the scissors.
13. Can you **snap** your fingers?
14. I set the table with a fork, a knife, and a **spoon**.

C. 1. Fetch the bone, Punkie.
2. Punkie, go and get the newspaper.
3. Find the shoe, Punkie.
4. Take the leash in your mouth.
5. Find the toy.
6. Don't chase the car.
D. 1. penny
2. toonie
3. dime
4. quarter
5. loonie
6. nickel

Review 1

A. 1. road ; toad ; load
2. like ; bike ; hike ; Pike
3. game ; came ; tame ; name
4. bake ; take ; cake ; lake ; rake
5. day ; Jay ; ray ; say ; way ; May
B. 1. vase   2. drum
3. jug   4. pin
5. nest   6. gate
7. mop   8. leaf
9. fan   10. yarn
11. hat   12. sock
13. web   14. six
15. cap
C. 1. tube   2. cake
3. log   4. bone
5. pole   6. hive
7. tent   8. fish
9. cube   10. rake
11. five   12. hand
D.

y	l	w	g	w	t	r	a	y	q	x	p	z	p	z	s
x	w	e	k	x	a	h	i	x	p	d	w	f	e	k	d
f	h	h	i	c	i	x	t	a	b	k	o	p	r	i	b
l	t	p	a	i	l	k	e	f	c	x	c	l	o	c	k
a	w	l	o	z	s	i	v	r	i	u	o	a	v	d	c
g	l	a	s	s	t	h	t	o	d	s	r	t	f	m	i
z	t	y	m	o	o	d	u	w	b	l	u	e	m	i	x
p	y	x	s	t	v	o	j	m	e	i	n	f	c	k	b
s	n	a	k	e	e	n	r	o	e	d	e	j	n	b	r
p	w	o	o	r	x	b	e	a	n	e	k	a	i	a	o
o	c	w	f	x	i	c	e	q	x	j	q	u	w	q	o
o	j	s	p	w	e	e	d	y	u	w	y	w	e	u	m
n	b	z	i	e	h	l	k	o	i	a	f	h	q	a	c
v	l	d	r	e	a	m	s	r	x	l	r	l	c	b	o
e	v	s	w	k	t	h	t	s	h	v	u	t	r	e	e
w	h	z	d	w	c	x	j	b	p	r	i	z	e	x	g
o	j	o	w	g	p	e	z	i	g	x	t	g	a	g	o
g	r	a	s	s	x	v	h	q	c	o	s	z	m	d	x

Answers

E. 1. . ; T   2. ? ; A
   3. . ; T   4. . ; I
   5. ? ; A   6. ! ; E
   7. . ; I   8. ! ; E

F. 1. The car (drove) down the highway.
   2. The bird (laid) the eggs in the nest.
   3. Mom (bakes) great cakes at home.
   4. Tom (walks) to school every day.
   5. She (likes) to (take) the dog for a walk.

G. 1. B   2. G
   3. C   4. D
   5. E   6. F
   7. A

H. (Individual answers)

10 The Treasure Chest

A. (Suggested answers)
   1. Rob heard about a sunken ship in Sharaz.
   2. They decided to search for the sunken treasure.

B. 1. Ch ; ch ; ch ; ch   2. Sh ; sh ; sh
   3. Th ; th ; th ; th ; th
   4. wh ; wh ; wh ; wh ; wh ; wh ; wh

C. 1. whiskers   2. thick
   3. ship   4. chest
   5. Peach   6. moth

D. 1. dogs   2. mats
   3. acorns   4. desks
   5. ships   6. tables
   7. foxes   8. girls
   9. rulers   10. lakes
  11. boats   12. roads
  13. toys   14. trees
  15. flowers   16. plants
  17. rugs   18. flags
  19. boys   20. masks

E. 1. horse   2. cow
   3. rabbit   4. dog
   5. kangaroo   6. pig
   7. chicken   8. goose
   9. cat   10. deer

11 A Visit to the Farm

A. 1. It is about different kinds of farms.
   2. They visited a dairy farm.
   3. He used big machines.

B.   Arnie's farm is far from the market. Every day, Arnie works very hard. He turns the soil, which is sometimes called dirt. When there are lots of worms in the soil, it is healthy. There are also lots of animals

on the farm. Some are horses and others are pigs, from which Arnie gets pork to sell at the market.

C. 1. Mark
   2. Ottawa
   3. Venus
   4. Mrs. Smith
   5. Sun
   6. Punkie
   7. Portland Drive
   8. Mars
   9. Canada Day
  10. Sunday
  11. The Gap
  12. Charlotte's Web
  13. Deer Lake
  14. May

D. 1. English
   2. Spanish
   3. France
   4. Hungarian
   5. Romanian
   6. Italian
   7. Greek

E. 1. ITALIAN   2. SPANISH   3. HUNGARIAN

12 Out on the Road

A. 1. A   2. F
   3. E   4. D
   5. C   6. B

B. **Clown**: town ; brown ; flowers ; crown
   House: hound ; blouse ; couch ; mouse ; sound
   Snowman: grow ; blow ; row ; glow ; rainbow ; low

C. six streetlights ; four cars
   ten flowers ; two boys
   five bicycles ; seven trees
   nine parking meters ; three trucks

D. 1. G   2. F
   3. B   4. H
   5. A   6. D
   7. C   8. E

13 The Coin Collection

A. 1. David has a coin collection.
   2. He has over three hundred coins.
   3. His first coins were from Italy.
   4. Many people have given him coins for gifts.
   5. He has coins from all over the world.
   6. David's favourite coin is one from Sri Lanka.

7. His favourite coin is large and heavy.

8. A Chinese coin has a hole in the centre.

B. 1. loyal   2. coin
3. boy   4. joy
5. point   6. soy
7. annoy   8. boil
9. toy   10. Oil

C.   (Answers will vary.)

D. 1. crying   2. breezy
3. tired   4. little
5. damp   6. big
7. hard   8. dirty

14   Making Blueberry Muffins

A. 1. muffins   2. wet
3. blueberries   4. egg
5. 400°F

B. 1. cook   2. book
3. look   4. cookbook
5. fool   6. pool
7. cool   8. drool

C. 1. is   2. are
3. is   4. is
5. are   6. are
7. are   8. am
9. is   10. is

D. 1. cold   2. short
3. thin   4. wet
5. sad   6. healthy
7. white   8. brave
9. answer

15   A Balloon Ride

A. 1. It was a sunny morning. ; F
2. T
3. The balloon was in the park. ; F
4. The balloon lifted off slowly. ; F

B. 1. half   2. talk
3. stalk   4. walk
5. calf   6. palm

C. 1. lamb
2. crumb
3. thumb
4. limb

D. 1. are   2. has
3. build   4. live
5. consists   6. breed

E. 1. hot ; cold   2. early ; late
3. best ; worst ;
calm ; windy
4. opened ; closed ;
up ; down

F.   (Individual writing)

16   Autumn

A. 1. season
2. summer
3. fall
4. beautiful
5. because
6. colour
7. ground
8. carpet
9. hike
10. animals
11. woods
12. fawns
13. woods

B. 1. Autumn follows summer.
2. They change colour and fall to the ground.
3. We find them in woods near cities.
4. Another name for autumn is fall.
5. Winter comes after autumn.

C. 1. fawn   2. jaw
3. straw   4. auto
5. saw   6. Autumn
7. saucer   8. yawn

D. 1. The <u>tired</u> boys rested under the <u>shady</u> tree.
2. He put a <u>big</u> book into a <u>small</u> bag.
3. The <u>friendly</u> nurse is helping the <u>sick</u> girl.
4. The <u>old</u> man is talking to the <u>young</u> child.
5. She picked a <u>red</u> apple from the <u>tall</u> tree.
6. The <u>black</u> puppy is playing with a <u>red</u> ball.

E.   (Individual writing)

F. 1. S   2. H
3. A   4. A
5. S   6. A
7. A   8. A
9. H

17   All about Plants

A. 1. They start as a seed.
2. They usually plant them in the garden or the yard.
3. They cover it with soil.
4. It takes a few weeks for shoots to sprout.

Answers

B.

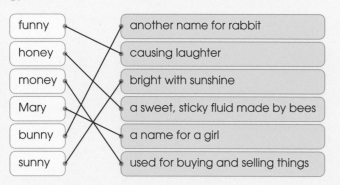

funny	another name for rabbit
honey	causing laughter
money	bright with sunshine
Mary	a sweet, sticky fluid made by bees
bunny	a name for a girl
sunny	used for buying and selling things

C. 1. Why   2. try
   3. fly   4. shy
   5. my

D.

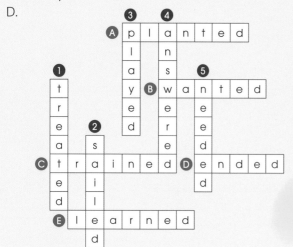

E. 1. December
2. September
3. February
4. October
5. January
6. June
7. August
8. November
9. March
10. May
11. July

18   Penguins

A. 1. Antarctica ; Africa ; Australia
2. Blue Fairy
3. 40 cm
4. Emperor
5. fish ; squid ; shrimp
6. female penguin ; male

B.   **SOFT c:** city ; circus ; cent
      HARD c: create ; cake ; clown ; cook

SOFT g: giant ; gym ; gem ; giraffe
HARD g: gate ; grow ; goose ; girl

C.
1. write — wrote
2. drink — thought
3. ring — drank
4. think — rang
5. drive — left
6. leave — drove

D. 1. eat   2. go
   3. try   4. swim
   5. lose   6. make

E.

Review 2

A. 1. oceans   2. small
   3. plates   4. chew
   5. whole   6. length
   7. weigh   8. smell
   9. pitches   10. breathing

B.   David and his friend, Judy, are going to visit the Hockey Hall of Fame in downtown Toronto, Canada. It is in a large building not far from Union Station, where the friends are taking the subway from Mississauga to Toronto.

There are so many exciting exhibits at the Hockey Hall of Fame. There are pieces of equipment worn by famous hockey players, like Wayne Gretzky. The Stanley Cup, which is awarded to the top hockey team each year, is sometimes on display there.

The children want to see the first mask that was worn by Jacques Plante and some of the old hockey uniforms from years gone by. Maybe, if they're lucky, they might see a visiting hockey player.

The last thing David and Judy go to see is all the statistics of players who broke many records over the years. Players like Gordie Howe, Jean Beliveau, and Wayne Gretzky changed the game of hockey forever.

C.   Canada ; largest ; North America ; ten ; three ; Nunavut ;

four ; three ; Maritime ; three

D. 1. is   2. like
    3. plays   4. studied
    5. takes   6. have
    7. laughs   8. is
    9. fixed   10. am

E.   (Individual writing)

F. 1. sale   2. sea
    3. pear   4. mail
    5. blue   6. vane

G. 1. large   2. cry
    3. tiny   4. run
    5. hop   6. sad

H. 1. bright   2. dry
    3. clean   4. close
    5. happy   6. heavy

I. 1. e   2. i
    3. e   4. i
    5. i   6. i
    7. e   8. e
    9. i   10. e
    11. e   12. e
    13. e   14. i
    15. e